Victory in The Storm

A GUIDE TO DEFEATING

DISCOURAGEMENT AND DEPRESSION

Sandra Hastings

MaxHoltMedia

© 2015 **Sandra Hastings**
Fourth Printing
Previous Edition (COUNTERATTACK) © 2007

Scripture quotations are from the King James Version (KJV) of the Bible

Published by MaxHoltMedia
303 Cascabel Place, Mount Juliet, TN 37122
www.maxholtmedia.com

Cover design by: Max Holt Media
Cover Photoi: ID 18063067 © Iakov Filimonov | Dreamstime.com

ISBN-13: 978-0-9966104-9-0

DEDICATION

Dedicated with love and appreciation to the two dear friends who helped and encouraged me through the deepest valley of my life.

Praise for
VICTORY IN THE STORM

"Sandy Hastings does not write from the perspective of Christian theory. Instead, she writes from Christian experience...her own Christian experience. The principles she shares in this volume have been proven in the ups and downs of her own walk as a missionary, wife, mother, counselor, and woman who has learned the lesson of total dependence on the Lord. Don't simply read this book. Breathe it."

Dr. Gib Wood, Missionary/Pastor,
Rheinland Baptist Church
Landstuhl, Germany

"In *Victory In The Storm*, Sandy Hastings has taken a great trial from her life and turned it into something helpful to others and glorifying to the Lord. Many women (and men) are plagued by the problem of depression...clinical (physically related), emotional, Spiritual. Sandy's testimony of

God's healing through His Word will be beneficial to anyone suffering from depression – for their friends and families, and for counselors of depressed individuals."

Mina Oglesby, Song Writer, Singer,
and Speaker
Chattanooga, TN

"One day I picked up this book, *Victory In The Storm*, and couldn't put it down. I thank God the He gave Sandy the desire and the strength to write. I had been struggling with discouragement and depression for some time. As I fight Satan with the word of God and not of myself, I know I will have victory. Thank you for writing this book."

David Collins, Business Proprietor
El Paso, TX

"I read *Victory In The Storm* the first time as a resource to use in helping others. But when I became discouraged and was facing depression, I pulled *Victory In The Storm* off the shelf and read it through with different eyes. I found it to be very helpful for me personally, especially working through the verses given. I now keep *Victory In The Storm* handy as a resource to help others and for myself. We are all susceptible to Satan's attacks and *Victory In The Storm* is a great weapon because it helps us to understand what God has supplied us with to stand against the wiles of the devil."

Phyllis Brakeen, Missionary wife,
Siberia

"Worry does not empty tomorrow of its sorrows; it empties today of its strength."

Corrie Ten Boom

CONTENTS

"My eye is not on the density of the fog, but on the living God, who controls every circum-stance of my life."

George Mueller

AUTHOR'S NOTES

I went to the mission field as a young wife and mother convinced I knew the Lord and how to live life for Him. I had great intentions, but much to learn. Among other things, the Lord chose depression to be part of my learning experience. As I began to come out of the dark, hopeless place I had been, I saw multitudes of women struggling in that same darkness. My heart went out to them and I wanted to share what God had taught me. Energized by this desire, the Lord lead me to write the first version of "Victory in the Storm".

The Lord was always there protecting, teaching and providing for my needs. He sent special people to help me. I am extremely thankful for Rev. L.E Holmes and his dear wife Edna. They invested countless hours with not only my husband and me, but also with our children as I struggled through the darkness. They did not claim to have all the answers, but they gave us God's Word wrapped in love and understanding.

This book has been revised and reprinted several times, and continues to be used by the Lord still today. It has also been translated into German, Russian, and Romanian. Depression is not limited to any particular age, culture, gender or social standing. It can happen to anyone, and although the causes vary, the dark sense of hopelessness and despair is the same. In this book, I share my testimony and an outline on what being a new creature in Christ means. Knowing and claiming personal possession of these truths will transform your spiritual life and bring you victory over depression.

FOREWORD

I am sure Sandy wasn't thinking of identifying with others when she was struggling with depression, but only of survival. By the grace of God, she not only survived but developed a greater love for God and His Word.

Sharing such a painful experience and revealing one's deep emotions is not an easy thing. However, each time Sandy tried to lay the book aside, the Lord brought her face to face with someone in deep need fighting depression, and the urgency of finishing what was started was renewed. **Victory In The Storm** is a very practical look at discouragement and depression and is easy to relate to. Many have asked for copies of this book while it was just stacks of handwritten notes.

Her desire in sharing this book is to glorify God for what He has done for her and to be a help to others who are experiencing depression. That desire will be fulfilled, for many have already been helped as Sandy has counseled with women individually and in groups when speaking at ladies meetings in churches. I'm thankful already for what the Lord will do with this little book. The help that many are praying for is going to be found for them in **Victory In the Storm**.

Edna Holmes, Pastor's Wife
Grapevine, Texas

1. "YE HAVE NOT CHOSEN ME BUT I HAVE CHOSEN YOU..."

In God's grace He drew me to himself, when by faith, I was saved at the age of ten. Even at this early age the Lord's hand was guiding my life. Being raised an only child, my parents and I were very close and shared most everything together.

However, they were not saved during this time and, therefore, could not understand spiritual matters. In spite of this, my desire to know the Lord and to be used of Him seemed to grow. I did not understand it, but there were moments in time that caused me to realize God had a definite plan for my life.

My parents taught me to be independent and self-reliant; these are desirable qualities. But, mixed with my strong will, they would prove to be a hindrance in my Christian life. By the end of high school, though still not sure what the Lord wanted for my life, I entered nurse's training.

During the following two years, I was faced with death on a day to day basis in my work. I could see the reality of Job 24:22, *"No man is sure of life."*

"... it is even a vapor, that appeareth for a little time and then vanished away." (James 4:14).

With more determination than ever I knew I wanted my life to count for the Lord. In all my sincerity I began to plan how I could serve Him. I often followed my own initiative and planning rather than the leadership of the Holy Spirit.

I had met Thomas Hastings my senior year in high school, and we dated through our early college days. We married upon my graduation from nurse's training in 1966.

Before marriage, Tom had already surrendered to preach and I was looking forward to the ministry. However, two months after we were married, the Holy Spirit burdened both our hearts and we surrendered to be missionaries. It was almost unbelievable to me. This was not my plan. In my mind, missionaries were super-spiritual people that have a special relationship with God. I was anything but that, and certainly did not feel capable of such service. However, as John 15:16 says, He had chosen me, I had not chosen Him. He knew what He would do with my life, and how He would carry out the purpose He had planned from the beginning.

Use these two pages to record how you feel about God having 'chosen you.' (Ephesians 1:4) Is this truth a reality in your life? If so how has that reality impacted your journey through YOUR storm? List additional scripture references that are helping you.

(YOUR NOTES)

2. "ALL THINGS WORK TOGETHER..."

In 1967, my husband and I enrolled in Baptist Bible College. We were eager to learn about the Lord and how we could most effectively serve Him. At this point I had accepted His will for us to be missionaries, however, my stubborn will was still often in command.

During the first year, I attended classes full-time and worked part-time as a Registered Nurse. My responsibilities increased when mid-year, my husband became Pastor of a little country church.

The next three years of our school life were very full: my husband continued to pastor for two years and taught half-days in a Christian School, and two of our three children were born.

Somehow, as my activity and the demand on my energy increased, I began to neglect my personal time with the Lord. Even as Jesus spoke to Martha in Luke 10:40-42, I became concerned about many things and neglected the most needful.

Upon graduation, we entered a new phase of our life. My husband began traveling across the country presenting the field of Germany to many churches. As they were led of the Lord to support us, we gained the funds needed to go to the mission field. It was a hectic time and the first real testing ground for the things we had been taught in school. In fifteen months we had raised our support and, with much expectation, made our way to West Germany.

Our first year and a half were extremely busy as we attended language school, worked with an American military church, and our third child was born.

In 1974, we moved to Koblenz where our German work was to be established. During the next four years, there was no let up in the demands on my time and energy. Days were filled with translating lessons, teaching ladies' and children's meetings and working on music for the church. With three children in school, there was always some activity that needed attention.

Due to our location, our home became a stopover for many pastors, other missionaries and just lonesome military families wanting fellowship. As the hours became more and more crowded, pressure began to mount.

However, I still believed I could handle any situation or task. I prayed, read my Bible, and many times took my needs and concerns to the Lord: but my confidence was in myself, not in Him.

1 Corinthians 10:12 says, *"Wherefore let him that thinketh he standeth take heed lest he fall."* Truly I was headed for a fall.

As time progressed, our life's pace continued to pick up speed. Guests in our home became almost constant while our work grew, bringing with it added activity. It seemed fatigue became a constant companion. Because we cannot separate the physical, spiritual, and emotional parts of our being, every part began to be affected. Nothing seemed to function normally. At times demands of the moment forced me to continue.

My self confidence and endurance were being pushed beyond the limit. Fear and an unexplainable feeling of foreboding began to surface. Though I confided in no one, the Lord knew exactly where I was.

Even as Jeremiah 23:24 says, *"Can any hide himself in secret places that I shall not see him? Saith the Lord."*

My husband and I had much to learn about communication and our priorities in the work. Somehow, we had acquired the idea that the work was first, regardless of the needs in other areas of our life. We took time for the people and every need of the work, but little or no time for one another.

My *situation* seemed to peak during the last year on the field. Panic passed through me as I realized I was losing control for the first time in my life. My own sufficiency and strength had run out. The more I felt myself slipping, the harder I tried and the more resentful I became. I felt everything in my life was falling apart and I could not see at all that God was working all things together for my good (Romans 8:28). At this point, God in His great mercy, led my husband to bring us home on furlough. I thought the worst was over, but it had not even begun.

Do you feel overwhelmed with responsibilities or the expectations of others? Make a list of what these are. What things appear to NOT be working together in your journey through YOUR storm. What could God be trying to show you? List scripture references that are helping you.

(YOUR NOTES)

3. "THE PRIDE OF THINE HEART HATH DECEIVED THEE..."

The nights grew long and my sleep restless. My body ached with fatigue but my mind could not be still. It rushed back over the days recounting the work that was done and all the projects that did not get finished. It seemed I could hear Satan, as he is described in Revelation 12:10, accusing me before the throne day and night. I felt as the scripture says in Deuteronomy 28:67, *"In the morning thou shalt say, 'would God it were even!' And at even, thou shalt say, 'would God it were morning!'"*

Satan in his cunning way seemed to attack from every direction. A sense of helplessness increased as old doubts resurfaced, minor irritations became major problems, and new temptations arose. I was overcome with feelings of guilt, inferiority and a lack of self-worth. A strong desire to escape began to occupy my thoughts. At times, I even toyed with the idea of suicide. I thought, *"Oh my God, am I so sinful? Have you utterly forsaken me? Where are you, Lord?"*

Slowly, my broken, shattered emotions began to seep with bitterness and resentment. I found myself lashing out in anger to the Lord and to those around me. *"It's not fair! I have given my whole life to the Lord: given up my ambitions, and desires. I had even left my homeland and struggled to adjust in a foreign country. I had worked and done the best I could – how could this happen to me?"*

I had not yet realized much of my service had been out of fear, and not love. My idea of God was not of a loving, merciful Father, but rather, a powerful, angry Creator waiting to punish me for every mistake. Therefore, I worked to win His acceptance and stay His hand of wrath.

In times of quiet, my mind drifted back over the years. I remembered two distinct instances that were clearly warnings from the Lord.

Once, an older and wiser missionary wife warned me to slow down, to take time for myself and my own needs. I listened, but just did not relate it to me. You see, until now I was never unstable or had bouts with depression. My life was full, busy and satisfying. On another occasion, a friend, who was also a pastor's wife, cautioned me concerning the fast pace I kept. I shrugged it off, after all, she was older than I and had some health problems.

I was healthy and strong, and had always maintained a hectic schedule in our ministry. Nothing could be left out. I did not realize that my vision was blurred by pride. *"Thy pride deceived thee."* (Obadiah 1:3). I did not heed the scripture in Proverbs 12:15, *"But he that hearkeneth unto counsel is wise."*

It is amazing how limited our spiritual vision can be. I had no idea the lessons the Lord was going to teach me, nor the blessing He had prepared. I did realize He was refining the vessel He had chosen (Isaiah 48:10).

In the weeks and months that followed, my husband realized I could not cope with the demands of the mission field. Therefore in 1979, after nine years of service, we resigned as missionaries.

Use this space to record how Pride has affected you and how God is helping you deal with it on your journey through YOUR storm. Make a list of those things you have "sacrificed" for God. When we are struggling with pride, who is at the center of our thoughts? (1 John 2:16) List additional scripture references that are helping you.

4. "YE DO ERR NOT KNOWING THE SCRIPTURES..."

Can you relate to any of the preceding accounts? More Christian women than ever before are finding themselves at various stages of depression. Is this some new dilemma or disease? Definitely not!

The Word tells us in Ecclesiastes 1:19, *"...there is no new thing under the sun."* This is certainly true concerning depression. Many great men of the Bible experienced it. Moses, in Numbers 11:15, had sank into despair over the sins of the children of Israel.

Elijah, in 1 Kings 19:4, asked the Lord to take his life. In great distress, Job said he was weary of life in Job 10:1. Even the disciples on different occasions felt defeated, rejected, afraid and wanted to give up.

However, depression does seem to be at an all time high in our society today. The causes vary from physical illness, death of a loved one, financial

19

crisis, a personal traumatic experience, or extreme fatigue.

But perhaps one of the greatest underlying causes for Christians, is the lack of reading and knowing God's Word. *"Jesus answered and said unto them, ye do err, not knowing the scriptures, nor the power of God."* (Matthew 22:29)

Every Christian is engaged in a battle, but not with flesh and blood. Ephesians 6:12 says that we are fighting against the *"rulers of darkness and spiritual wickedness in high places."* Their leader, Satan, is cunning, deceitful, vicious and powerful.

Once we are saved, our souls are not in danger (John 10:27-28), but we can be attacked physically and emotionally. *"Be sober, vigilant; because your adversary the devil, as a roaring lion, walketh about, seeking whom he may devour"* (1 Peter 5:8). Christ even told Peter, *"Simon, Simon, behold Satan hath desired to have you, that he may sift you as wheat..."*

How then can we fight against this enemy? Ephesians Six describes our spiritual armor, including our shield of faith. When we are discouraged and depressed, our faith is definitely weak, causing our shield to be lowered. Furthermore, the Word is described as our sword. If we neglect His Word, we have no weapon wherewith to fight. In this unprotected State we are vulnerable to every attack from Satan.

His attack may not be obvious, but rather subtle even as it was with Eve in the Garden of Eden. He shakes us to our very foundation as he questions, *"Hath God said, 'nothing can separate you from the love of God?'"* (Romans 8:38); *"Hath God said, 'whosoever shall call upon the name of the Lord shall be saved?'"* (Romans 10:13)

We are tormented in agony as our minds are flooded with unbelief and fear. Because we are so overwhelmed by these feelings, we do not realize this is sin. *"For whatsoever is not of faith is sin,"* (Romans 14:23); *"nor is it of God,*

"For God hath not given us the spirit of fear, but of power and of love, and of a sound mind."

If we continue to indulge in these fearful, unbelieving thoughts mixed with guilt, we will find ourselves falling headlong into a lonely whirlpool of despair. As it begins to spiral downward, it increases in swiftness and intensity. The more we doubt, the greater the fear, the heavier the guilt.

We cry out in desperation for help before we are totally broken, *"Oh Lord, God of my Salvation, I have cried day and night before thee: For my soul is full of troubles, and my life draweth nigh unto the grave. I am counted with them that go down in to the pit: I am as a man that hath not strength"* (Psalms 88:1,3,4).

There is help. *"Fear thou not: for I am with thee; be not dismayed, for I am thy God: I will help thee, yea I will uphold thee with the right hand of my righteousness"* (Isaiah 41:10).

We must face the reality of sin in our lives. It is this sin that is stealing our joy and power, and causing us to be immobilized in our Christian life. It is of vital importance, however, that we realize the sin is not the temptation, but the yielding. Once it is recognized and confessed, the Lord's forgiveness is sure and He begins to restore our soul.

Though the battle has turned, the fighting is not over. Satan never gives up so easily. After we have confessed our sin and are forgiven, he may try to defeat us with recurring feelings of guilt. It is useless to try and reason it away. Only the Scriptures can defeat this attack and give us the security we need. 1 John 1:9 tells us that, *"If we confess our sins, He is faithful and just to forgive us our sins and to cleanse us from all unrighteousness."*

Because God cannot lie (Titus 1:2), we can be sure we are forgiven. *"I, even I, am he that blotteth out your transgressions for mine own sake, and will not remember thy sins"* (Isaiah 43:25).

Therefore, if our sins are confessed,

they are forgiven and forgotten. If forgotten, then the guilt we feel is not from the Holy Spirit, but from the father of lies, Satan himself (John 8:44). If we continue to listen to his lies, our condition will worsen until we can no longer cope with reality or be active in the Lord's work. In time, some may, in total defeat, take their own life as a means of escape.

This is a tremendous waste and a deep grief to our Lord. Hebrews 5:15-16, tells us we have a high priest who was tempted in all points as we. That means he has experienced the very temptation we battle. Yet He sinned not and had victory over Satan in every area. He tells us we can boldly ask for grace and help in time of need. There is perhaps no greater need than when we are being destroyed by discouragement and depression.

Christ has not only provided the way of salvation (John 14:6), and has endured every form of temptation without sinning, but has given every

born again believer the power to resist
the Devil (James 4:7). The ability to
resist comes through faith (1 Peter 5:9),
and faith comes from the Word of God
(Romans 10:17).

We *can* have the victory over
depression and defeat all the various
attacks from Satan. Our power is in
God's Word. As we read it, mediate on
it and claim it for our own personal
lives, our faith will increase. Even as
Hebrews 10:23 says, we must *"hold fast
to the promises of God without wavering;
for He is faithful that promised."*

If the victory was based on our
ability to outwit Satan, we would be lost.
But the battle is the Lord's and we have
only to read His Word, accept it as truth,
and apply it to our own personal lives.
(Zechariah 4 :6)

We often seek help and relief from
our mates, family, or friends. But there
is no one that can give us the victory
and peace we so desire except the
Lord. *"Thou wilt keep him in perfect
peace whose mind is stayed on thee,*

25

because he trusteth in thee." (Isaiah 26:3).

You may find yourself in the same dilemma as I did. Where should I read? Where do I begin? The Lord led me to the Book of Psalms.

As I began to read, David through the leadership of the Holy Spirit, expressed the very feelings I felt. The Scriptures related to me. Slowly the promises of forgiveness and mercy became reality, bringing with them peace and comfort.

This did not happen overnight, nor even in a few days. It had taken a long time for me to get in this *state*. Therefore, the healing would also take time. I had to read every day; frequently spending much time during the day putting the Word of God into my heart and mind.

Sometimes this did not mean reading many chapters but repeating the same verses over and over until they began to be reality to me. As this process continued, slowly I would, with

26

David, praise the Lord and gain victory in my life. Our God is faithful when He promises to hear the broken hearted, and to heal up their wounds! (Psalms 147:3)

Since that time, I have met so many other Christian and non-Christian women suffering from defeat and depression. Therefore, it is my desire to share what the Lord, through His Word, has done for me in the hope that it will be a help and encouragement to others.

In the following pages, verses from Psalms are categorized the way they were a blessing to me. As you read them, think on them and claim them for your life. They are God's promises to YOU.

Write out what God's Word means to you. How has it effected your life as you journey through YOUR storm? Did you know the Bible is God's love letter to you? Consider that thought as you read the next section of this book. Colossians 3:16 List additional scripture references that are helping you.

5. **THE NEED OF OUR HEARTS**

PSALM

13:1   "How long wilt thou forget me, O LORD? forever? how long wilt thou hide thy face from me?"

22:1,2   "My God, my God, why hast thou forsaken me? Why art thou so far from helping me, and from the words of my roaring? O my God, I cry in the daytime, but thou hearest not; and in the night season, and am not silent."

22:6   "But I am worn..."

22:11   "Be not far from me; for trouble is near; for there is some to help."

22:15   "My strength is dried up..."

22:19   "But be not thou for from me, O Lord: O my strength, haste thee to help me."

25:4   "Shew me thy ways, O Lord; teach me thy paths."

38:6   "I am troubled; I am bowed down greatly; I go morning all the day long."

38:8   "I am feeble and sore broken."

38:9,10 "Lord, all my desire is before thee; and my groaning is not his from thee. My heart panteth, my strength faileth me:"

40:11   "Withhold not thou thy tender mercies from me, O Lord: let thy loving kindness and thy truth continually preserve me."

40:13   "Be pleased, O Lord to deliver me: O Lord, make haste to help me."

55:4-6 "My heart is sore pained within me, and the terrors of death are fallen upon me. Fearfulness and trembling are come upon me, and horror hath overwhelmed me. And I said, Oh that I had wings like a dove! for then would I fly away and be at rest."

61:1,2 "Hear my cry, O God; attend unto my prayer. From the end of the earth will I cry unto thee, when my heart is overwhelmed: lead me to the rock that is higher than I."

63:1 "O God thou art my God, early will I seek thee: my soul thirsteth for thee: my flesh longeth for thee in a dry and thirsty land, where no water is."

69:1-3 "Save me, O God; for the waters are come in unto my soul. I sink in deep mire, where there is no Standing: I am weary of my crying: my throat is dried: mine eyes fail while I wait for my God."

69:5 "O God, thou knowest my foolishness: and my sins are not hid from thee."

69:16,17 "Hear me, O Lord; for thy loving kindness is good: turn unto me according to the multitudes of thy tender mercies. And hide not thy face from thy servant; for I am in trouble: hear me speedily."

69:20 "Reproach hath broken my heart; and I am full of heaviness: and I looked for some to take pity, but there was none; and for comforters, but I found none."

70:1 "Make haste, O God, to deliver me; make haste to help me, O Lord."

70:5 "But I am poor and needy; make haste unto me, O God: thou art my help and my deliverer; O Lord, make no tarrying."

71:1-4 "I cry unto God with my voice: and he gave ear unto me. In the day of my trouble I sought the Lord: my sore ran in the night, and ceased not: my soul refused to be comforted. I remembered God, and was troubled: I complained, and my spirit was overwhelmed. Thou holdest mine eyes waking: I am so troubled that I cannot speak."

86:1 "Bow down thine ear, O Lord, hear me; for I am poor and needy."

88:1-4 "O Lord God of my salvation, I have cried day and night before thee: Let my prayer come before thee: incline thine ear unto my cry; For my soul is full of troubles: and my life draweth nigh unto the grave. I am counted with them that go down in to the pit: I am as a man that hath no strength:"

88:6-9 "Thou hast laid me in the lowest pit, in darkness in the deeps. Thy wrath lieth hard upon me and thou hast afflicted me with all thy waves. Selah. Thou hast put away mine acquaintance far from me, thou hast made me an abomination unto them: I am shut up and I cannot come forth. Mine eye mourneth by reason of affliction. Lord I have called daily upon thee, I have stretched out my hands unto thee."

88:15 "I am afflicted and ready to die..."

102:1,2 "Hear my prayer, O Lord, and let my cry come unto thee. Hide not thy face from me in the day when I am in trouble; incline thine ear unto me: in the day when I call answer me speedily."

119:107 "I am afflicted very much: quicken me, O Lord, according unto thy word."

130:1-3 "Out of the depths have I cried unto thine ears be attentive to the voice of my supplications. If thou Lord, shouldest mark iniquities, O Lord, who shall stand?"

141:1   "Lord, I cry unto thee: make haste unto me: give ear unto my voice, when I cry unto thee."

142:1-6 "I cried unto the Lord with my voice; with my voice unto the Lord did I make my supplication. I poured out my complaint before him; I shewed before him my trouble. When my spirit was overwhelmed within me, then thou knewest my path. In the way wherein I walked have they privily laid a snare for me refuge failed me; no man cared for my soul. I cried unto thee, O Lord; I said, thou art my refuge and my portion in the land of the living. Attend unto my cry; for I am brought very low: deliver me from my persecutors; for they are stronger than I."

143:4   "Therefore   is   my   spirit overwhelmed   within   me;   my   heart within me is desolate."

143:6 "I Stretch for my hands unto thee: my soul thirsteth after thee, as a thristy land. Selah."

143:7 "Hear me speedily, O Lord: my spirit faileth: hide not thy face from me, lest I be like unto them that go down unto the pit."

143:9-11 "Deliver me, O Lord from mine enemies: I flee unto thee to hide me. Teach me to do thy will; for thou art my God: thy spirit is good; lead me into the land of uprightness. Quicken me, O Lord, for they name's sake: for they righteousness' sake bring my soul out of trouble. And of thy mercy cut off mine enemies, and destroy all them that afflict my soul; for I am thy servant."

Use the next two pages to write out the verses in Psalms that express how you feel. Start recording the Needs of Your Heart as you journey through YOUR storm. Write out other verses that are helping you at this time.

(YOUR NOTES)

6. FORGIVENESS

PSALM

25:7　"Remember, not the sins of my youth, nor my transgressions: according to thy mercy remember thou me for thy goodness' sake, O Lord."

25:11　"For thy name's sake, O Lord, pardon mine iniquity, for it is great."

25:18　"Look upon mine affliction and my pain; and forgive all my sins."

32:5　"I acknowledge my sin unto thee, and mine iniquity have I not hid. I said, I will confess my transgressions unto the Lord: and thou forgavest the iniquity of my sins. Selah."

38:18　"For I will declare mine iniquity; I will be sorry for my sin."

51:1-2 "Have mercy upon me, O God, according to thy lovingkindness;

according unto the multitude of thy tender mercies blot out my transgressions. Wash me thoroughly from mine iniquity, and cleanse me from my sin."

51:7,9,10 "Purge me with hyssop, and I shall be clean: wash me, and I shall be whiter than snow. Hide thy face from my sins, and blot out all mine iniquities. Create in me a clean heart, O God; and renew a right spirit within me."

51:16,17 "For thou desirest not sacrifice; else would I give it: thou delightest not in burnt offering. The sacrifice of God are a broken spirit; a broken and a contrite heart, O God thou will not despise."

86:5 „For thou, Lord, art good, and ready to forgive; and plenteous in mercy unto all them that call upon thee."

103:10,12 "He hath not dealt with us after our sins; nor rewarded us according to our iniquities. As far as the east is from the west, so far that he removed our transgressions from us."

130:4,5 "But there is forgiveness with thee, that thou mayest be feared. I wait for the Lord, my soul doth wait, and in his word do I hope."

Use this page and the next to record the areas in your life where you struggle with Forgiveness. Do you suffer with feelings of guilt? If so, write the verses from the preceding list that show you God's forgiveness. Why does He forgive us? (Ephesians 1:7) List the additional scripture references that are helping you.

(YOUR NOTES)

7. SECURITY

PSALM

4:8 "I will both lay me down in peace, and sleep: for thou, Lord only makest me dwell in safety."

5:11 "But let all those that put their trust in thee rejoice: let them ever shout for joy, because thou defendest them: let them also that love thy name be joyful in thee."

7:10 "My defense is of God, which saveth the upright in heart."

9:9 "The Lord also will be refuge for the oppressed, a refuge in time of trouble."

17:8 "Keep me as the apple of the eye, hide me under the shadow of thy wings."

18:1,2 "I will love thee, O Lord my strength. The Lord is my rock and my fortress, and my deliverer; my God, my strength, in whom I will trust; my buckler..."

18:18b "...but the Lord was my stay."

18:31-33 "For who is God save the Lord? or who is a rock save our God? It is God that girdeth me with strength, and maketh my way perfect. He maketh my feet like hinds' feet, and satteth me upon my high places."

23:1 "The Lord is my shepherd; I shall not want."

27:1 "The Lord is my light and my salvation; whom shall I fear? The Lord is the strength of my life; of whom shall I be afraid."

27:13,14 "I had fainted, unless I had believed to see the goodness of the Lord in the Lord in the land of the living. Wait on the Lord: be of good courage, and he shall strengthen thine heart: wait, I say, on the Lord."

28:7,8 "The Lord is my strength and my shield; my heart trusted in him, and I am helped: therefore my heart greatly rejoiceth; and with my son will I praise him. The Lord is their strength, and he is the saving strength of his anointed."

29:11 "The Lord will give strength unto his people; the Lord will bless his people with peace."

31:2,3 "Bow down thine ear to me; deliver me speedily; be thou my strong rock, for an house of defense to save me. For thou are my rock and my fortress; therefore for thy name's sake lead me, and guide me."

31:19,20 "Oh how great is thy goodness, which thou hast laid up for them that fear thee; which thou hast wrought for them that trust in thee before the sons of men! Thou shalt hide them in the secret of thy presence from the pride of man: Thou shalt keep them secretly in a pavilion from the strife of tongues."

31:24 "Be of good courage, and he shall strengthen your heart, all ye that hope in the Lord."

32:7,8 "Thou art my hiding place, thou shalt preserve me from trouble; thou shalt compass me about with songs of deliverance. Selah."

33:18-20 "Behold, the eye of the Lord is upon them that fear him, upon them that hope in his mercy; to deliver their soul from death, and to keep them alive in famine. Our soul waiteth for the Lord: he is our help and our shield."

34:4 "I sought the Lord, and he heard me, and delivered me from all my fears."

34:7 "The angel of the Lord encampeth round about them that fear him, and delivereth them."

34:10 "The young lions do lack, and suffer hunger: but they that seek the Lord shall not want any good thing."

34:15 "The eyes of the LORD are upon the righteous, and his ears are open unto their cry."

34:17-19 "The righteous cry, and the LORD heareth, and delivereth them out of all their troubles. The LORD is nigh unto them that are of a broken heart; and saveth such as be of a contrite spirit. Many are the afflictions of the righteous: but the LORD delivereth him out of them all."

37:4,5 "Delight thyself also in the LORD; and he shall give thee the desires of thine heart. Commit thy way unto the LORD; trust also in him; and he shall bring it to pass."

37:7   "Rest in the LORD, and wait patiently for him: fret not thyself because of him who prospereth in his way, because of the man who bringeth wicked devices to pass."

37:23,24   "The steps of a good man are ordered by the LORD; and he delighteth in his way. Though he fall, he shall not be utterly cast down: for the LORD upholdeth him with his hand."

37:28   "For the LORD loveth judgment, and forsaketh not his saints;"

37:39   "But the salvation of the righteous is of the LORD: he is their strength in the time of trouble."

39:7   "And now, Lord, what wait I for? my hope is in thee."

40:1-3 "I waited patiently for the LORD; and he inclined unto me, and heard my cry. He brought me up also out of an horrible pit, out to the miry clay, and set my feet upon a rock, and established my goings. And he hath put a new song in my mouth, even praise unto our God: many shall see it, and fear, and shall trust in the LORD."

40:5 "Many, O LORD my God, are thy wonderful works which thou hast done, and thy thoughts which are to us-ward: they cannot be reckoned up in order unto thee: if I would declare and speak of them, they are more than can be numbered."

40:17 "But I am poor and needy; yet the Lord thinketh upon me: thou art my help and my deliverer; make no tarrying, O my God."

42:5 "Why art thou cast down, O my soul? And why art thou disquieted in me? hope thou in God: for I shall yet praise him for the help of his countenance."

SANDRA HASTINGS

46:1 "God is our refuge and strength, a very present help in trouble."

48:14 "For this God is our God for ever and ever: he will be our guide even unto death."

50:15 "And call upon me in the day of trouble: I will deliver thee, and thou shalt glorify me."

55:16,17 "As for me, I will call upon God; and the LORD shall save me. Evening, and morning, and at noon, will I pray, and cry aloud: and he shall hear my voice."

55:22 "Cast thy burden upon the LORD, and he shall sustain thee: he shall never suffer the righteous to be moved."

59:9 "Because of his strength will I wait upon thee: for God is my defense."

61:1,2 "Hear my cry, O God; attend unto my prayer. From the end of the earth will I cry unto thee, when my heart is overwhelmed: lead me to the rock that is higher than I."

62:2 "He only is my rock and my salvation; he is my defense; I shall not be greatly moved."

62:5-7 "My soul, wait thou only upon God; for my expectation is from Him. He only is my rock and my salvation: he is my defense; I shall not be moved. In God is my salvation and my glory: the rock of my strength, and my refuge, is in God."

73:22-26 "So foolish was I, and ignorant: I was as a beast before thee. Nevertheless I am continually with thee: thou hast holden me by my right hand. Thou shalt guide me with the counsel, and afterward receive me to glory. Whom have I in heaven but thee? and there is none upon earth that I desire beside thee. My flesh and my heart faileth: but God is the strength of my heart, and my portion for ever."

84:5   "Blessed is the man whose strength is in thee: in whose heart are the ways of them."

86:6,7 "Give ear, O LORD, unto my prayer; and attend to the voice of my supplications. In the day of my trouble I will call upon thee: for thou wilt answer me."

91:4   "He shall cover thee with his feathers, and under his wings shalt thou trust: his truth shall be thy shield and buckler."

94:22 "But the LORD is my defense; and my God is the rock of my refuge."

103:13,14 "Like as a father pitieth his children, so the LORD pitieth them that fear him. For he knoweth our frame; he remembereth that we are dust."

105:4,5 "Seek the LORD, and his strength: seek his face evermore. Remember his marvelous works that he hath done;"

116:1,2 "I love the LORD, because he hath heard my voice and my supplications. Because he hath inclined his ear unto me, therefore will I call upon him as long as I live."

118:6 "The LORD is on my side; I will not fear: what can man do unto me?"

118:14 "The LORD is my strength and song, and is become my salvation."

119:114 "Thou art my hiding place and my shield: I hope in thy word."

121:1-3 "I will lift up mine eyes unto the hills, from whence cometh my help.

My help cometh from the LORD, which made heaven and earth. He will not suffer thy foot to be moved: he' that keepeth thee will not slumber."

125:2 "As the mountains are round about Jerusalem, so that LORD is round about his people from henceforth even for ever."

126:5,6 "They that sow in tears shall reap injoy. He that goeth forth and weepeth, bearing precious seed, shall doubtless come again with rejoicing, bringing his sheaves with him."

128:1 "Blessed is every one that feareth the LORD; that walketh in his ways."

138:8 "The LORD will perfect that which concerneth me: thy mercy, O LORD, endureth for ever: forsake not the works of thine own hands."

139:1-16 "O LORD, thou hast

searched me, and known me. Thou knowest my downsitting and mine uprising, thou understandest my thought afar off. Thou compassest my path and my lying down, and art acquainted with all my ways. For there is not a word in my tongue, but, lo, O LORD, thou knowest it altogether. Thou hast beset me behind and knowledge is too wonderful for me; it is high, I cannot attain unto it. Whither shall I go from thy spirit? Or whither shall I flee from thy presence? If I ascend up into heaven, thou art there: if I make my bed in hell, behold, thou art there. If I take the wings of the morning, and dwell in the uttermost parts of the sea; Even there shall thy hand lead me, and thy right hand shall hold me. If I say, Surely the darkness shall cover me; even the night shall be light about me. Yea, the darkness hideth not from thee; but the night shineth as the day: the darkness and the light are both alike to thee. For thou hast possessed my reins; thou hast covered me in my mother's womb. I will praise thee; for I am fearfully and wonderfully made: marvelous are thy works; and that my soul knoweth right well. My substance was not hid from thee, when I was made in secret, and curiously wrought in the lowest parts of the earth. Thine eyes did see my substance, yet being imperfect; and in thy book all my members were written, which in continuance were fashioned, when as yet there was none of them."

144:2 "My goodness, and my fortress; my high tower, and my deliverer; my shield and he in whom I trust; who subdueth my people under me."

145:18,19 ..The LORD is nigh unto all them that call upon him, to all that call upon him in truth. He will fulfill the desire of them that fear him: he also will hear their cry, and will save them."

Everyone has a need to feel safe and secure. Use this page and the next to record the needs you have in the area of Security. Using the preceding verses, write out those that speak personally to you about God's care. In what whys does God keep us secure? Why can you depend on God's care of you? 1 Peter 4;7 List the additional scripture references that are helping you.

(YOUR NOTES)

8. MERCY

PSALM

6:2 "Have mercy upon me, O LORD: for I am weak: O LORD, heal me; for my bones are vexed."

9:13 "Have mercy upon me, O LORD..."

27:7 "Hear, O LORD, when I cry with my voice: have mercy also upon me, and answer me."

30:10 "Hear, O LORD, and have mercy upon me: LORD, be thou my helper."

31:9,10 "Have mercy upon me, O LORD, for I am in trouble: mine eye is consumed with grief, yea, my soul and my belly. For my life is spent with grief, and my years with sighing: my strength faileth because of mine iniquity, and my bones are consumed."

31:16 "Make thy face to shine upon thy servant: save me for thy mercies' sake."

41:10 "But thou, O LORD, be merciful unto me, and raise me up, that I may requite them."

51:1 "Have mercy upon me O God, according to thy lovingkindness: according unto the multitude of thy tender mercies blot out my transgressions."

57:1 "Be merciful unto me, O God, be merciful unto me: for my soul trusteth in thee: yea, in the shadow of thy wings will I make my refuge, until these calamities be overpast."

86:15 "But thou, O Lord, art a God full of compassion, and gracious, longsuffering, and plenteous in mercy and truth."

103:4 "Who redeemeth thy life

from destruction; who crowneth thee with lovingkindness and tender mercies;"

103:8 "The LORD is merciful and gracious, slow to anger, and plenteous in mercy."

103:11 "For as the heaven is high above the earth, so great is his mercy toward them that fear him."

103:17 "But the mercy of the LORD is from everlasting to everlasting upon them that fear him, and his righteousness unto children's children;"

116:5 "Gracious is the LORD, and righteous; yea, our God is merciful."

138:8 "The LORD will perfect that which concerneth me: thy mercy, O LORD, endureth for ever: forsake not the works of thine own hands."

God's mercy is His kindness, compassion, and tenderness with which He deals with sinful man. According to the previous verses, what has God assured you about His mercy? How have you experienced God's mercies in your life? (Ephesians 2:4) List additional scripture references that are helping you.

9. TRUST

PSALM

5:11   "But let all those that put their trust in thee rejoice:"

7:1 "O LORD my God, in thee do I put my trust: save me from all them that persecute me, and deliver me:"

9:10   "And they that know thy name will put their trust in thee: for thou, LORD, hast not forsaken them that seek thee."

11:1   "In the Lord I put my trust..."

13:5   "But I have trusted in thy mercy; my heart shall rejoice in thy salvation."

16:1   "Preserve me, O God: for in thee do I put my trust."

18:2   "The LORD is my rock, and

my fortress, and my deliverer; my God, my strength, in whom I will trust; my buckler, and the horn of my salvation, and my high tower."

18:30 "As for God, his way is perfect: the word of the LORD is tried; my buckler, and the horn of my salvation, and my high tower."

25:2 "O my God, I trust in thee:"

28:7 "The LORD is my strength and my shield; my heart trusted in him, and I am helped: therefore my heart greatly rejoiceth; and with my song will I praise Him."

31:1 "In thee, O LORD, do I put my trust; let me never be ashamed: deliver me in thy righteousness."

31:6 "...but I trust in the LORD."

31:14 "But I trusted in thee, O LORD: I said, Thou art my God."

32:10 "...but he that trusteth in the LORD, mercy shall compass him about."

34:8 "O taste and see that the LORD is good: blessed is the man that trusteth in Him."

34:22 "The LORD redeemeth the soul of his servants: and none of them that trust in Him shall be desolate."

36:7 "How excellent is thy lovingkindness, O God! therefore the children of men put their trust under the shadow of thy wings."

37:3 "Trust in the Lord..."

37:40 "And the LORD shall help them, and deliver them: he shall deliver them from the wicked, and save them, because they trust in Him."

40:4 "Blessed is that man that maketh the LORD his trust,"

52:8　"But I am like a green olive tree in the house of God: I trust in the mercy of God for ever and ever."

56:3,4　"What time I am afraid, I will trust in thee. In God I will praise His word, in God I have put my trust; I will not fear what flesh can do unto me."

56:11　"In God have I put my trust: I will not be afraid what man can do unto me."

62:8　"Trust in Him at all times; ye people, pour out your heart before Him: God is a refuge for us. Selah."

71:1　"In thee, O LORD, do I put my trust: let me never be put to confusion."

71:5　"For thou art my hope, O Lord GOD: thou art my trust from my youth."

73:28 "But it is good for me to draw near to God: I have put my trust in the Lord GOD, that I may declare all thy works."

91:2 "I will say of the LORD, He is my refuge and my fortress: my God; in Him will I trust."

115:11 "Ye that fear the LORD, trust in the LORD; he is their help and their shield."

118:8.9 "It is better to trust in the LORD than to put confidence in man. It is better to trust in the LORD than to put confidence in princes."

141:8 "But mine eyes are unto thee, O GOD the Lord: in thee is my trust: leave not my soul destitute."

143:8 "Cause me to hear thy lovingkindness in the morning: for in thee do I trust: cause me to know the way wherein I should walk; for I lift up my soul unto thee."

Trust requires a conscience choice, a deliberate act of my will. In what areas of my life do I need to trust God? According to the previous verses, what are the benefits of trusting Him? How are you learning to Trust the Lord more? Proverbs 3:5 List the additional scripture references that are helping you.

10. THANKSGIVING

PSALM

30:12 "To the end that my glory may sing praise to thee, and not be silent. O LORD my God, I will give thanks unto thee for ever."

75:1 "Unto thee, O God, do we give thanks, unto thee do we give thanks: for that thy name is near thy wondrous works declare."

92:1 "It is a good thing to give thanks unto the LORD, and to sing praises unto thy name, O most High:"

106:1 "Praise ye the LORD, O give thanks unto the LORD; for he is good: for his mercy endureth for ever."

118:29 "O give thanks unto the LORD; for he is good: because his mercy endureth for ever."

119:71 "It is good for me that I have

been afflicted; that I might learn thy statues."

136:1 "O give thanks unto the LORD; for he is good: for his mercy endureth for ever."

138:3 "In the day when I cried thou answeredst me, and strengthenedst me with strength in my soul."

139:14 "I will praise thee; for I am fearfully and wonderfully made: marvelous are thy works; and that my soul knoweth right well."

139:17,1 "How precious also are thy thoughts unto me, O God! how great is the sum of them! If I should count them, they are more in number than the sand: when I awake, I am still with thee."

Why should we be thankful to God? List those things, people and situations for which you are Thankful. Voice your thankfulness to God and to someone for at least one thing every day. Hebrews 13:15 List the additional scripture references that are helping you.

(YOUR NOTES)

11. PRAISE

PSALM

9:1,2   "I will praise thee, O LORD, with my whole heart; I will shew forth all thy marvelous works."

27:6   "And now shall mine head be lifted up above mine enemies round about me; therefore will I offer in his tabernacle sacrifices of joy; I will sing, yes, I will sing praises unto the LORD."

32:11   "Be glad in the LORD, and rejoice, ye righteous: and shout for joy, and ye that are upright in heart."

33:1   "Rejoice in the LORD, O ye righteous: for praise is comely for the upright."

34:1-3 "I will bless the LORD at all times: his praise shall continually be in my mouth. My soul shall make her boast in the LORD: the humble shall hear thereof, and be glad. O magnify the

73

LORD with me, and let us exalt his name together."

35:18 "I will give thee thanks in the great congregation: I will praise thee among much people."

44:8 "In God we boast all the day long, and praise thy name for ever."

56:10 "In God will I praise his word: in the LORD will I praise his word."

63:3 "Because thy lovingkindness is better than life, my ups shall praise thee."

68:19 "Blessed be the Lord, who daily loadeth us with benefits, even the God of our salvation."

69:30 "I will praise the name of God with a song and will magnify him with thanksgiving."

95:1,2 "O Come, let us sing unto the LORD: let us make a joyful noise to the rock of our salvation. Let us come before his presence with thanksgiving, and make a joyful noise unto him with psalms."

100:1,2 "Make a joyful noise unto the LORD, all ye lands. Serve the LORD with gladness: come before his presence with singing."

100:5 "For the LORD is good: his mercy is everlasting; and his truth endureth to all generations."

103:1,2 "Bless the LORD, O my soul: and all that is within me, bless his holy name. Bless the LORD, O my soul, and forget not all his benefits:"

105:1,2 "O give thanks unto the LORD; call upon his name: make known his deeds among the people. Sing unto him, sing psalms unto him: talk ye of all his wondrous works."

105:3 "Glory ye in his holy name: let the heart of them rejoice that seek the LORD."

107:2 "Let the redeemed of the LORD say so, whom he hath redeemed from the hand of the enemy:"

108:4 "For the mercy is great above the heavens: and thy truth reacheth unto the cloud."

109:30 "I will greatly praise the LORD with my mouth; yea, I will praise him among the multitude."

111:1 "Praise ye the LORD. I will praise the LORD with my whole heart, in the assembly of the upright, and in the congregation."

118:28 "Thou art my God, and I will praise thee: thou art my God, I will exalt thee."

135:3 "Praise the LORD; for the LORD is good: sing praises unto his name; for it is pleasant."

135:13 "Thy name, O LORD, endureth for ever; and thy memorial, O LORD, throughout all generations."

139:14 "I will praise thee; for I am fearfully and wonderfully made: marvelous are thy works; and that my soul knoweth right well."

145:2,3 "Every day will I bless thee; and I will praise thy name for ever and ever. Great is the LORD, and greatly be praised; and his greatness is unsearchable."

145:5 "I will speak of the glorious honor of thy majesty, and of thy wondrous works."

145:21 "My mouth shall speak the praise of the LORD: and let all flesh bless his holy name for ever and ever."

146:1,2 "Praise ye the LORD. Praise the LORD, O my soul. While I live will I praise the LORD: I will sing praises unto my God while I have any being."

147:1 "Praise ye the LORD: for it is good to sing praises unto our God; for it is pleasant; and praise is comely."

147:7 "Sing unto the LORD with thanksgiving; sing praise upon the harp unto our God:"

148:1 "Praise ye the LORD. Praise ye the LORD from the heavens: praise him in the heights."

148:13 "Let them praise the name of the LORD: for his name alone is excellent; his glory is above the earth and heaven."

150:6 "Let every thing that hath breath praise the LORD. Praise ye the LORD."

Reflect on the previous verses and list the things you can praise God for. What other things in your life can you praise Him for? (1 Peter 2:9) List the additional scripture references that are helping you.

(YOUR NOTES)

12. I CRIED UNTO THE LORD

"In my distress I cried unto the Lord and he heard me." (Psalms 120:2)

"Not only did he hear me but he brought me up also out of a horrible pit, out of the miry clay, and set my feet upon a rock and established my goings. And he hath put a new song in my mouth, even praise unto our God." (Psalms 40:2,3)

Today I must say, I am what I am by the grace of God. In the last few years since my major bout with depression, God's Word has come to mean more than ever before. There was a time in my life when I read it only because that is what Christians were suppose to do.

Today, I read it because it gives me what I need to cope with daily living, and it draws me closer to the Lord. Scriptures concerning Christian living are just like those for salvation. If we do not accept them personally they have no power in our lives.

As we read the promises of God, we must accept his Word and believe they are made for each one of us PERSONALLY. Claim them, stand firm with all confidence that what God has promised He will surely do. *"I have spoken it, I will also bring it to pass; I have purposed it, I will also do it."* (Isaiah 46:11)

I wish I could say the battle was over, never to be fought again. However, this is not the case. Satan will still try the same attack only from a different approach.

Now, however, I recognize it much quicker and from experience I know how to gain the victory. We must never make the mistake of thinking we are beyond any certain temptation.

False confidence in oneself can be the beginning of a fall. Satan never takes a vacation. But God knows our every need. *"It is of the Lord's mercies that we are not consumed, because his compassions fail not. They are new every morning..."* (Lamentations 2:23)

Today, I and my husband have returned to the field of Germany. Often times the situations have been difficult, but the Lord has taught us many lessons. He makes no mistakes. When He chose me before the foundation of the world, (Ephesians 1:4,5) He knew what it would take to break my stubborn will and how He would teach me the truths of His Word. *"The Lord hath chasten me sore: but he hath not given me over unto death. I shall not die, but live and declare the works of the Lord."* (Psalms 118:17,18)

Perhaps one of the most common temptations is in the area of self-worth. Thousands of people today, both saved and unsaved, are trying to find approval from others to affirm their own value. They invest millions of dollars in clothes, cosmetics, diets, jewelry and various fads, in an attempt to gain acceptance from others. This is evident in all age groups. Yet, these attempts result in short term success or complete failure.

Unconditional acceptance and love

can only be found in a personal relationship with Jesus Christ. This is ours to experience through accepting Christ as our personal Savior and learning to live in the position He gives us as God's children. John 1:12; 3:16.

The following outline is designed to help you understand that position. Each one of us is unique. God made only one exactly like you. You were not a mistake or an afterthought but formed by God for a definite purpose. As you read and study the following thoughts and scriptures, let them become reality in your life and accept all the Lord has given to you.

"According as his divine power hath given unto us all things that pertain unto life and godliness, through the knowledge of him that hath called us to glory and virtue: Whereby are given unto us exceeding great and precious promises: that by these ye might be partakers of the divine nature, having escaped the corruption that is in the world through lust." 2 Peter 1:3-4

(Use this page and the next to record those times when you have prayed (CRIED) unto the Lord and how He responded. You may even want to write out a prayer to God...praying as you write the words. List the additional scripture references that are helping you in the area of PRAYER.)

(YOUR NOTES)

13. OUR POSITION IN CHRIST

I. Consider our God
A. There is only one God
1. Isaiah 40:18 "To whom then will ye liken God? or what likeness will ye compare unto him?"
2. Isaiah 43:10,11 "...before me there was no God formed, neither shall there be after me. I, even I, am the LORD; and beside me there is no saviour."
3. Isaiah 40:25 "To whom then will ye liken me, or shall I be equal? saith the Holy One."
4. Isaiah 45:5,6 "I am the LORD, and there is none else, there is no God beside me: I girded thee, though thou hast not known me: That they may know from the rising of the sun, and from the west, that there is none beside me. I am the LORD, and there is none

else."

B. His tremendous power is beyond our comprehension
   1. Jeremiah 10:12 "He hath made the earth by his power, He hath established the world by his wisdom, and hath stretched out the heavens by His discretion."
   2. Jeremiah 10:10 "But the LORD is the true God, He is the living God, and an everlasting king:"
   3. Genesis 1:1 "In the beginning God created the heaven and the earth."
   4. Genesis 2:7 "And the Lord God formed man of the dust of the ground, and breathed into his nostrils the breath of life; and man became a living soul."
   5. Psalm 115:3 "But our God is in the heavens: He hath done whatsoever he pleased.

C. He is complete with all power within himself.

1. Psalms 135:6 "Whatsoever the LORD pleased, that did He in heaven, and in earth, in the seas, and all deep places."

2. Colossians 1:16-17 "For by him were all things created, that are in heaven, and that are in earth, visible and invisible, whether they be thrones. Or dominions, or principalities, or powers: all things were created by him, and for him: And he is before all things, and by him all things consist."

3. Hebrews 2:10 "For it became him, for whom are all things, and by whom are all things, in bringing many sons unto glory, to make the captain of their salvation perfect through sufferings."

4. Romans 11:36 "For of him, and through him, and to him, are all things: to whom be glory forever."

II. Keep the picture of this awesome creator, in your mind and ask yourself – BE HONEST – Do I know Him? Do I feel loved and accepted by Him?

A. Many problems develop because we are controlled by feelings and not my God's truth. We are plagued with thoughts such as, "I'm not as good as others are; Oh, God will do it for you but not for me. I am not worthy; I have failed so utterly, that God can't use me."

B. The key to changing these attitudes and feelings, is to realize that our total worth is in Jesus Christ. It is not in our abilities or accomplishments.

III. Our value from the human perspective

A. Many times the Lord urges us to be still.

1. Psalm 46:10 "Be still, and know that I am God."

2. Isaiah 30:15 "...in quietness and confidence shall be your strength."

B. In ourselves, we are unworthy.

1. Isaiah 64:6 "But we are all as an unclean thing, and all our righteousnesses are as filthy rags; and we all do fade as a leaf; and our iniquities, like the wind have taken us away."

2. Romans 7:18 "For I know that in me, that is in my flesh, dwelleth no good thing."

3. Romans 3:10 "As it is written, There is none righteous, no, not one:"

4. Romans 8:8 "So then they that are in the flesh cannot please God."

5. Hebrews 11:6 "But without faith it is impossible to please Him:"

C. We set our goals, many

SANDRA HASTINGS

times, without Consulting God.
When we fall short, we believe we
are failures and therefore of little
worth.

1. God does not promise
strength for all the goals and
desires of the flesh.

2. Because we have built our
worth on the wrong bases, it
begins to crumble.

D.   We may see the way others
treat us as an indication of our
worth.

1. Jesus was the very Son of
God, perfect and of infinite
worth, yet, He was rejected.
"He came unto his own and his
own received him not." John
1:11; Luke 23:18; Isaiah 53:3.
"He was mocked, ridiculed
and spat upon." Matthew
27:28-31.

2. Other people are also sinful,
opinionated and imperfect
beings with limited

knowledge. Therefore, their opinions are a poor bases for evaluating our own worth. 2 Corinthians 10:12 "For we dare not make ourselves of the number, or compare ourselves with some that commend themselves: but they measuring themselves by themselves, and comparing themselves among themselves are not wise."

IV. Our value from God's perspective

A. He knows all about us.

1. Psalm 103:14 "For he knoweth our frame; he remembereth that we are dust."

2. Psalm 139:1-3 "O LORD, thou hast searched me, and known me. Thou knowest my downsitting and mine uprising, thou understandest my thought afar off. Thou compassest my

path and my lying down, and are acquainted with all my ways."

3.Job 42:2 "I know that thou canst do every thing, and that no thought can be withholden from thee."

4. Matthew 6:8 "Be not ye therefore like unto them: for your Father knoweth what things ye have need of, before ye ask him"

B. We are created in His image.

Genesis 1:27,31 "So God created man in his own image, in the image of God created he him;

...And God saw every thing that he had made and, behold, it was very good."

C. Remember He does whatever pleases Himself.

1.Psalm 115:3 "But our God is in the heavens: he hath done whatsoever he hath pleased."

2. The plan of salvation and all that God gives us when we become His children is because it pleases Him. None of it is based upon our deserving it. Isaiah 43:7 "every one that is called by my name: for I have created him for my glory, I have formed him: yea, I have made him."

3. Ephesians 1:11 "In whom also we have obtained an inheritance, being pre-destinated according to the purpose of him who worketh all things after the counsel of his own will:"

Jesus said, *"And ye shall know the truth and the truth shall make you free. If the Son therefore shall make you free, ye shall be free indeed."* John 8:32,36

All of us grow up with certain beliefs about God, ourselves and the world around us. These beliefs are those things we are convinced of in our hearts and out of them come our attitudes, thoughts and feelings. Often these beliefs are not based on God's truth, but rather on traditions, superstitions, and man's faulty reasoning. They are lies.

For example, I may be convinced that I'm not really a sinner like others are, God could not love me, I'm not as valuable as someone else, or I don't deserve God's blessings. These lies are the roots from which various fears, insecurities and other faulty attitudes grow. If left unchanged, they will interfere with our fellowship with the Lord and can greatly limit our availability and Spiritual growth.

A thorough study of the topics listed in this next section will set you free! It will help you *"put off the old man and put on the new man."* Ephesians 4:22-24. Remember, these truths are reality, and our rejection of, or lack of faith in, does not nullify them!

V. The believer's position in Christ
A.   A new CREATURE

"Therefore, if any man be in Christ, he is a new creature, old things are passed away; behold, all things are become new." 2 Corinthians 5:17

"For we are his workmanship, created in Christ Jesus unto good works, which God hath before ordained that we should walk in them." Ephesians 2:10

B.   FORGIVEN – Our sins are forgiven in and through Jesus Christ.

"In whom we have redemption through his blood, the forgiveness of sins, according to the riches of his grace" Ephesians 1:7

"And you, being dead in your sins and the uncircumcision of your flesh, hath he quickened together with him, having forgiven you all trespasses; Blotting out the handwriting of ordinances that was against us, which was contrary to us, and took it out of the way, nailing it to his cross;" Colossians 2:13-14

It is important for us to admit and repent of our sins. It is our new position in Christ that makes it possible for us to be forgiven.

C. SANCTIFIED – We are set apart by God for His service. The believer belongs to the Lord and is His servant.

"By the which will we are sanctified through the offering of the body of Jesus Christ once for all. And every priest standeth daily ministering and offering oftentimes the same sacrifices, which can never take away sins: But this man, after he had offered one sacrifice for sins for ever, sat down on the right hand of God; From henceforth expecting till his enemies be made his footstool. For by one offering he hath perfected for ever them that are sanctified." Hebrews 10:10-14

"Wherefore Jesus also, that he might sanctify the people with his own blood, suffered without the gate." Hebrews 13:12

Spiritual growth is learning to live a holy, sanctified life. "Having therefore these promises, dearly beloved, let us cleanse ourselves from all filthiness of the flesh and spirit, perfecting holiness in the fear of God." 2 Corinthians 7:1

"But grow in grace, and in the knowledge of our Lord and Savior Jesus Christ. To him be glory both now and forever. Amen." 2 Peter 3:18

We will be completely holy when we get to heaven. "Beloved, now are we the sons of God, and it doth not yet appear what we shall be: but we know that, when he shall appear, we shall be like him; for we shall see him as he is." 1 John 3:2

D.   RIGHTEOUS – The believer

has no righteousness of his own, and is therefore given the perfect righteousness of Jesus Christ.

"For he hath made him to be sin for us, who knew no sin; that we might be made the righteousness of God in him." 2 Corinthians 5:21

"And be found in him, not having mine own righteousness, which is of the law, but that which is through the faith of Christ, the righteousness which is of God by faith." Philippines 3:9

"For if by one man's offence death reigned by one; much more they which receive abundance of grace and of the gift of righteousness shall reign in life by one, Jesus Christ." Romans 5:17.

E. JUSTIFIED – The Greek word translated "justified" is actually a judicial word and it means more than forgiven, more than acquitted. It means because of Christ, the Father sees us as if we had NEVER SINNED. We are declared righteous; free from quilt and punishment before God the Father.

"For all have sinned, and come short of the glory of God; being justified freely by his grace through the redemption that is in Christ Jesus." Romans 3:23-24

"Therefore we conclude that a man is justified by faith without the deeds of he law." Romans 3:28

"For he hath made him to be sin for us, who knew no sin; that we might be made the righteousness of God in him." 2 Corinthians 5:21

F.   ADOPTED into God's family for eternity

"But as many as received him, to them gave he power to become the sons of God, even to them that believe on his name:" John 1:12

"For ye are all the children of God by faith in Christ Jesus." Galatians 3:26

"But when the fullness of the time was come, God sent forth his Son, made of a woman, made under the law, to redeem them that were under the law, that we might receive the adoption of sons. And because ye are sons, God hath sent forth the Spirit of his Son into your hearts, crying, Abba, Father. Wherefore thou art no more a servant, but a son; and if a son, then an heir of God through Christ." Galatians 4:4-7

G.   ACCEPTED – Through Jesus Christ we are made acceptable to God the Father.

"To the praise of the glory of his grace, wherein he hath made us accepted in the beloved." Ephesians 1:6

"Ye also, as lively stones, are

built up a spiritual house, an holy priesthood, to offer up spiritual sacrifices, acceptable to God by Jesus Christ." 1 Peter 2:5

H. INDWELLED by the Holy Spirit – The Holy Spirit is given to every believer.

"In whom ye also trusted after that ye heard the word o truth, the gospel of your salvation in whom also, after that ye believed, ye were sealed with that Holy Spirit o promise. Which is the earnest of our inheritance until the redemption of the purchased possession, unto the praise of his glory." Ephesians 1:13-14

"But ye are not in the flesh, but in the Spirit, if so be that the Spirit of God dwell in you. Now if any man have not the Spirit of Christ, he is none of his." Romans 8:9

"Hereby know we that we dwell in him, and he in us,

103

because he hath given us of his Spirit." 1 John 4:13

"Who hath also sealed us, and given the earnest of the Spirit in our hearts." 2 Corinthians 1:22

The believer becomes the temple of the Holy Spirit.

"Know ye not that ye are the temple of God, and that the Spirit of God dwelleth in you? If any man defile the temple of God, him shall God destroy; for the temple of God is holy, which temple ye are." 1 Corinthians 3:16-17

The Holy Spirit is given to guide, protect, comfort, empower and convict me of sin.

The Holy Spirit will never leave the believer. However, through rebellion or deliberate sin, the believer can quench or grieve Him.

"And grieve not the Holy Spirit of God, whereby ye are

sealed unto the day of redemption." Ephesians 4:30

"Quench not the Spirit." 1 Thessalonians 5:19

When we grieve or quench the Spirit, it lessens our spiritual power and hinders our fellowship with the Lord. The problem can be remedied by confession and repentance. Our Lord is then faithful to forgive us.

"If we confess our sins, he is faithful and just to forgive us our sins, and to cleanse us from all unrighteousness." 1 John 1:9

I. ETERNAL LIFE – The believer has eternal life and cannot ever be lost again.

"For God so loved the world, that he gave his only begotten Son, that whosoever believeth in him should not perish, but have everlasting life. He that believeth on the Son hath everlasting life:

and he that believeth not the Son shall not see life; but the wrath of God abideth on him." John 3:16,36

"My sheep hear my voice, and I know them, and they follow me: And I give unto them eternal life; and they shall never perish, neither shall any man pluck them out of my hand. John 10:27-28

"For the wages of sin is death; but the **gift** of God is eternal life through Jesus Christ our Lord." Romans 6:23

"In hope of eternal life, which God, that cannot lie, promised before the world began;" Titus 1:2

"And this is the record, that God **hath given** to us eternal life, and this life is in his Son. He that hath the Son hath life; and he that hath not the Son of God hath not life. These things have I written unto you that believe on the name of the Son of God; that ye may know that ye have eternal life, and that ye may believe on the name of the Son of God." 1 John 5:11-13

The new position we as believers have is a divine gift. It is:

1. Based in Jesus Christ
2. Immediate
3. Spontaneous
4. Unchangeable
5. Not connected to man's experience or feelings
6. Complete
7. Not dependent on man's behavior or his ability to earn them
8. Eternal

"I know that, whatsoever God doeth, it shall be forever: nothing can be put to it, nor any thing taken from it: and God doeth it, that men should fear before him." Ecclesiastes. 3:14

We can trust our Lord and rest safe and secure in the position He has given to us. Knowing these truths is the first step. Then we must chose with our will to claim them true for us personally. Now we can move forward by the power of the Holy Spirit trusting our Lord to do what He has promised. It is Christ living through us. "I can do all things through Christ which strengthenth me." Philippians 4:13

The air is charged with a sense of urgency as our Lord's return draws closer. Let us defeat Satan, by accepting our position in Christ and draw from the power promised to us. Christ has already won the victory!

You are special in the sight of God: created, loved, redeemed and called to serve Him. Let me encourage you even as Paul, to forget those things which are behind and reach forth unto those things which are before, pressing toward the mark for the prize of the high calling of God in Christ Jesus.

(Use these next two pages to record your thoughts about your position in relation to Christ. Based on your particular journey, where do stand with Him or where do you NEED to stand with Him? The journey through YOUR storm will be smoother when you have that in perspective. List additional scripture references that are helping you.)

(YOUR NOTES)

EPILOGUE

This small book has been in circulation for thirty-three years. In the last few years women have often asked, "So what has happened since the last chapter?" So now, I will try to briefly answer this question.

We returned to Germany in 1983. Through these past years, the Lord has carried us through a variety of experiences. My major encounter with depression was over, but I had to use self discipline and maintain my fellowship with the Lord to keep it from returning. Relying on the truths presented in the previous outline has proved to be my strength for every day and in every situation.

Raising three teens in Germany brought its own set of challenges and lessons. The German church we started in 1984 and organized in 1994, brought many opportunities for spiritual growth. While helping the various people through their crises and experiences,

111

God often showed me the areas of my life that still needed to be changed.

In the process of time, we took each of our three children back to America to further their education. This was a particularly painful time for me. It felt like my heart was being torn out, yet, I knew it was the Lord's will.

Again, His grace proved sufficient. Slowly, the pain grew less and the Lord began to fill the empty space with new opportunities and ministries.

Sometimes, when children leave home, women are tempted to feel their meaningful life is over. That is not true. It is not the end but rather merely a change of season. For me, it allowed time and energy for ministries I had previously not been able to do.

Then came the weddings with all their preparations, excitement and even tears. They brought me a mixture of emotions. I felt hope and excitement for the future but also the sad pangs of turning loose and allowing our precious children to be on their own.

As our first grandchild was born in September 1991, I was overwhelmed with how quickly time had passed. It seemed somehow unfathomable that our little girl had just given birth to her own child!

Now, twenty-four years later, we are blessed with twelve grandchildren, and every one of them is a very special and unique person.

I mentioned in chapter two that my husband and I had much to learn about communication and priorities. These lessons were not easy. We had to first recognize our own pride and stubbornness. It was necessary for God to humble each of us, that we might humble ourselves before one another. The Lord is patient and merciful, doing all things well!

We have now been married forty-nine years and I'm happy to tell you that our marriage is sweeter than ever before. Communication is still not always easy, but we have learned it is worth the time and effort it takes to work things out.

The marriage relationship must be nourished and cared for on a regular bases. It cannot wait until the children are grown or a professional goal has been reached. If your list of priorities has your marriage relationship anywhere other than second only to the Lord, it is out of order.

Humanly speaking, the largest part of my life has been lived. My husband and I have been in full time ministry for forty-eight years. We have had trials, heartaches, sickness and a variety of those things that God uses to teach us our dependence on Him, and His faithfulness to us.

We have also experienced many blessings, much joy and even some miracles. In the last few years, the Lord has expanded our ministry. As doors open, we travel to other mission fields teaching God's truths and encouraging His servants. It is exciting to experience a growing reality of who God is, and to see Him working, even in the small details of everyday life.

In my early years, I did not realize that living in close fellowship with God was the most exhilarating and exciting life possible. I am thankful my Lord never stopped working on me, and even now, He continues to teach me and draw me closer to His side. However much time He allows me to live, my desire is to bring Him glory in whatever way He chooses.

I can testify to the truth of Romans 8:28-29 *"And we know that all things work together for good to them that love God, to them that are called according to his purpose. For whom he did foreknow, he also did predestinate to be conformed to the image of his Son, that he might be the firstborn among many brethren."*

God is not finished with me yet. I am still under construction, but one day in His kingdom, I will be perfect.

(Use this page to record some thoughts about your own journey through 'Your Storm.' I would love to hear your story about how my words and especially God's Word have helped you. You can email me at ..... sandy.hastings@gmx.de.)

ABOUT THE AUTHOR

Sandra Hastings was born in Pueblo Colorado, in September 1946. She graduated from Southern Colorado State College with a A.A. in Nursing in 1966, and shortly thereafter, married Thomas Hastings. They both attended and graduated from Baptist Bible College in 1970. In 2000 Sandra earned an M.A. in theology..

Sandra and Thomas have been in full-time ministry for forty-eight years; forty- two of which were spent ministering with German nationals in their country.

Sandra is a published author and has had the privilege of speaking to women's groups in various countries in Europe, Russia, Okinawa, and in the United States.

She and Thomas have been married for forty-nine years and continue to live in Germany. They have three children and twelve grandchildren

Made in the USA
San Bernardino, CA
04 February 2016